Mother of Abominations
Witchcraft Dreamscapes

A Collection of Poems and Art by

Orlee Stewart

Edited by Mishlen Linden

BLACK MOON PUBLISHING
Cincinnati Ohio, USA

Black Moon Manifesto

It is the Will and mission of Bate Cabal/Black Moon to effectively manifest unique and insightful occult Works for the esoteric community in a manner that is unfettered by commercial considerations.

Acknowledgements: thank you to the collectors of my artwork who's support and contributions to the book helped preserve and arrange this collection spanning fifteen years of images, including: Jenna Laflèche, Michel Beriault, Rex Parsons, Nemo Theaphilus, Tasha Menary, and Mishlen Linden.

Published by Black Moon Publishing, LLC
Cincinnati Ohio USA

BlackMoonPublishing.com

blackmoonpublishing@gmail.com

Design and layout by
Jo Bounds of Black Moon

ISBN: 979-8-9853204-5-9

United States • United Kingdom • Europe • Brazil • Australia • India • Japan

CONTENTS

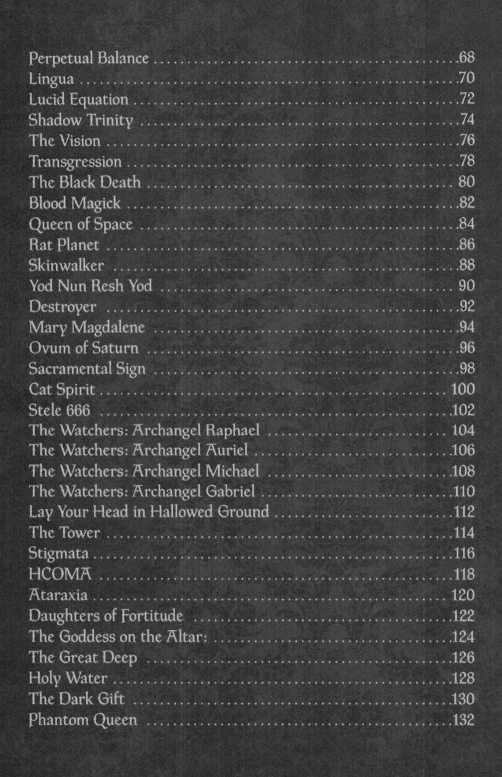

FOREWORD

Welcome!
You have arrived at the Door. The Door of Orlee Stewart.

In this assemblage of her visions is a chance to go farther, know more and hear their ancient speech. Beyond these pages is a powerful, radical and sacred space. Her unique perception lies within, enclosed for all to see. Her world is before you and all you have to do is turn a page! Transparent and invisible realities are made from the sacred flesh and visions therein. They will, if you wish, condense themselves into you. Here, the Unknowable is made known. Trancing through this book will give you the feeling of being in a ritual, and that is proper, for it is a ritual book.

Expand what you see and you will navigate a world of both dreams and nightmares. You may forget yourself (don't worry, there is a ritual for that).

These are the keys to her Queendom. And they contain the evokations to enter it. Because there are no mere images here. She embraces the Unknown, seer and mistress, the Mother of Abominations. Here is a silent world that screams soundlessly. Every image releases another wound to pass beyond. The entranceways she has opened with her images break free from the pages and enter your heart.

Remember that you are entering a divine and alien world. Broken things come here to heal, and the merely curious can see, but never touch.

A warning;

You are entering a world you have turned your face from long ago. Aeons ago. It is right to fear it for ego abhors change, and it will change you. Look at yourself before you turn the pages any farther. When you are done, look at yourself again.

For those who would risk a touch in order to know your own Nightside dwelling-place, let me share my experience with you:

I began by seeing these as surrealist artworks. Pages on a book. Surreal and sublime, her dreamscapes touched me with a longing I had not expected. Her places, peopled with her Selves, were real.

They gave birth to themselves through these very images and I took my time going through them. Deeper and deeper they drew me in until I found myself standing in her world. I could see the life teeming within it, weaving through it, alive with their own inner visions. I cast my eyes about the luminous landscape. It came in 3-D and I was filled with a strange reverence.

Then a new feeling burst inside me. A flower, blood-red, bloomed inside me. It remained in constant motion as the petals fell and the fruit formed before me. In this alien world was the fruit of wisdom!

What you do next is your own choice.

I chose to eat it, and it grew inside me. As her spirits became a part of me, I became larger, knowing what they knew. The gift of understanding them became a part of me. My former self began to shed. I had grown too large for my own cloth to fit. And I realized we are ALL serpents in Eve's garden. But we have ALL taken a bite from this fruit, in part, and we are One.

The fruits come in many forms and colors, and there is one for you.

Bless her!

– Mishlen Linden

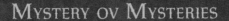

MYSTERY OV MYSTERIES

All aboard the ship of fools to the world of lost light
Our blood is a map to the future and past, drawn as the stars align.
We take our seat among the flames in the sacred house of God.
May our flight be no heavier than the weight of Maat's feather
As we slip through the vast cosmic beyond.

The spells unfold with each word as she spoke.
Mysteries lost into black holes.
Our self has been divided enough,
Let us find the demons we have lost.
May we arise in our brilliant burning.
A beautiful mourning from that which haunts our souls.

Sacred space, hear my deepest cries.
Know that I am pregnant with the abyss,
Naked and trembling upon her altar.
May the sky unveil her hidden language,
The script of flesh upon a world of illusions.
Veiled self I awaken your brilliant dark matter,
Open my heart to your mysteries and I will devour your pearls.

She told me that the universe can wait
And we watched it dance around the dirty bones upon the floor
Spiraling into decaying aeons yet to be born
She calls us each to find our seats in the craft destined for what is
unknown.

We are the dreaming and the living
We have taken our seats in the West
In this place there is no time
As we embark upon a journey
Across the illusion that is a lie.

Mystery ov Mysteries, acrylic on wood panel, 2013.

My Demon Mother

I invoke thee, mother of the corrupted womb.
Lilith, eyes gleaming with the reflection of the moon.
We call unto you through the corroding veil of yesod,
I am Eve, the innocent one who has lost her way.
I am she who's heart is girt with the serpent.
The mysteries of your desires are ripe,
We dare to taste your forbidden fruit.

Oh garden of flesh,
Let my body decay into you.
May I return to the garden's bloom.
Have we found ourselves lost in exile?
Will the gate be opened by an unseen hand or my own?
Shall we return to the illusion of a perfected genesis?
All these questions and no answer, for we are the garden.
The energy of humanity is the fruit of cosmic forces.

Mother of vampires,
You haunt the shadow work of the magician.
Mother of the dead children who were never born.
Lilith, the beauteous monster who broken men fear.
I come before you, naked and pure.
Cleansed by the waters of my own tears for this dying world.
I come before you as I was born and eat of the tree.
The all devourer who sacrifices everything
And thus becomes one with all.

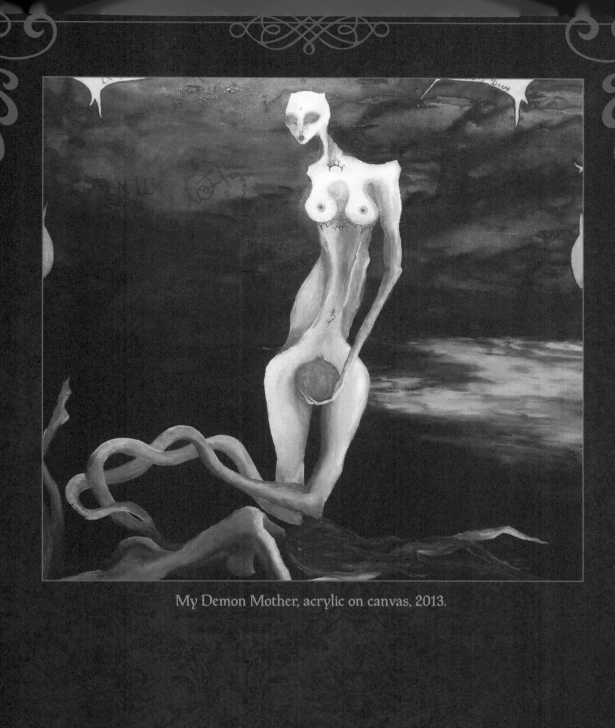

My Demon Mother, acrylic on canvas, 2013.

The Hour of Virtue

Far away in a foreign land
and maybe in another dimension,
Where there is no time.
There is a woman who spends eternity
Waiting for the perfect moment.
She died in this space and never even knew that it was impossible.

Here we are in the place where existence is an illusion.
The hour is upon us.
The hour draws nigh to bleed every last drop
Of spirit into the sweet nectar of life.

The bees are swarming upon the flowers.
The sacred rose in the garden of desolation.
In this hour all is returned to the hive
as we have found the pollen of your blooms.

There is no answer here.
No divine perfection to await upon.
All is here in our bodies
As grains of sand are infinite worlds.
As each possibility exists to define its opposite.
The hour is upon us now.

The Hour of Virtue, acrylic on canvas, 2012.

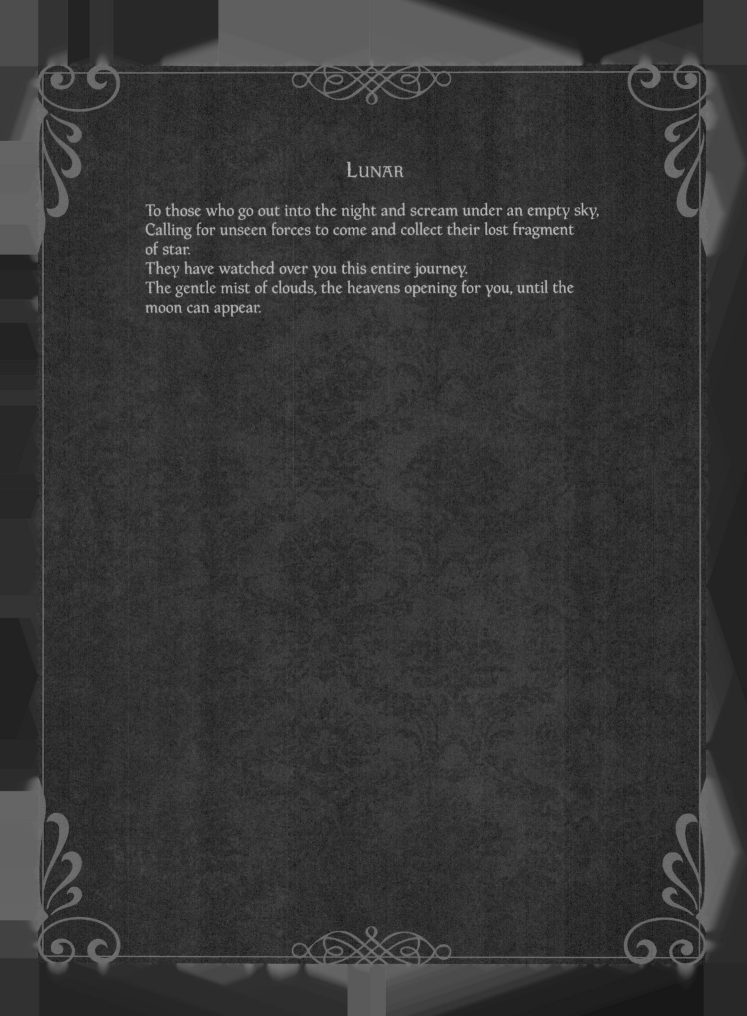

Lunar

To those who go out into the night and scream under an empty sky,
Calling for unseen forces to come and collect their lost fragment
of star.
They have watched over you this entire journey.
The gentle mist of clouds, the heavens opening for you, until the
moon can appear.

Lunar, acrylic on canvas, 2012.

Going to Seed

The Mother of Abominations reveals her offspring,
Each a new world of obscure landscapes.
The first revealed a curious feast
The vampiric creature has become a new breed.
No longer feeding upon the mortal coil.
Bodies twisted into obscure shapes
Form the organic synthesis of blood into foliage.
A planet where the trees are bone,
Their roots have become veins into the clotted soil.
Here they lounge amidst the vapors of an unclaimed sky.
Their synthesis is a biological evolution which transcends the flesh,
Transmuting Saturn into Venus.
A new world among many others which grows from the horrors of the
blind harlot.
From the blood of the saints which pours deeply from her goblet.
Each world connected by the rivers which unite their bleeding.
Dissolving into dark waters so we may become one in them.
Their seeds remain to sow the garden once again.

Going to Seed, acrylic on canvas, 2012.

Life in the Dead World

This space was created by the wish upon a star
In the highest peak of your subjective reality.
In the valley of the ruins of a crumbled city.
Citadels fallen and shadow remains.

Herein the life force of earth becomes the energy of stars.
The dance of death reveals herself
As parasites feed on the shells of their host.
They forage the earth to find ghosts of the divine.

A magick spell unfolded on that night
When the only light remained was that consecrated orb.
A bride of the night feasted on the thorns
Which released an egg for a new world to be formed.

Life in the Dead World, acrylic on canvas, 2012.

Imperium

The majesty of chaos.
A combination of the will and which can not be described.
Lounging on the edge of the abyss,
With the sky a brilliant turbulence.
The beetle shining as it flies,
Wings spreading from the cavernous mind.
Reflecting the light of moonlit skies.
This power is reclaimed through the arching of the gateway.

Imperium, 2011 acrylic on canvas.

CARRION FLOWER

The seen and the unseen.
Prophets have revealed themselves
Through the passing times.
Each one through a variation of forme.
There is no gender to the infinite source that contains all.
Once discarded and obscured from their own power.
Something terrifying waits beyond what was allowed to grow.
That dark feminine secret, hidden beyond the occult of misogyny.
Her flesh rots in the garden and the sacred rose has become a carrion
flower.

Carrion Flower, acrylic on canvas, 2011.

Aetas Intereo

Passing through the valley, going deeper.
Further into the unknown parts of your heart.
Through the veil of life.
Into the place before the beginning and the end.
Herein scrapes the shells of our society, creatures frolicking in blood.

Putrid decay.
Primordial pools.
Nature begins to regrow from the scraps.
The source of light is not lost.
Guiding the way to a new Pangaea.
Maybe we will leave our pain behind, although we carry it well.

Aetas Intereo, acrylic on canvas, 2011.

Forma Caelestis

Calling down the source of all information.
Illuminates the Orphic serpent upon the auric egg.
Let the spells be spoken,
As the cosmos unfolds in never ending light.
I call you, part of myself that is all things.
That which creates new life from chaos.
Forces that weave infinities to pass.
The shadow of the deep and the expanse of space.
By the two that are opposing which divide light and darkness.
By the one that contains all.
By the zero that holds every possibility.
Two, one, zero: the egg, the serpent and the void.
IAO Deus Insania
The spell is spoken and the abyss is crossed.
Forma Caelestis
The crossing over of geometrical shapes,
Non-forms into flesh.
Channeling the current of creative process.

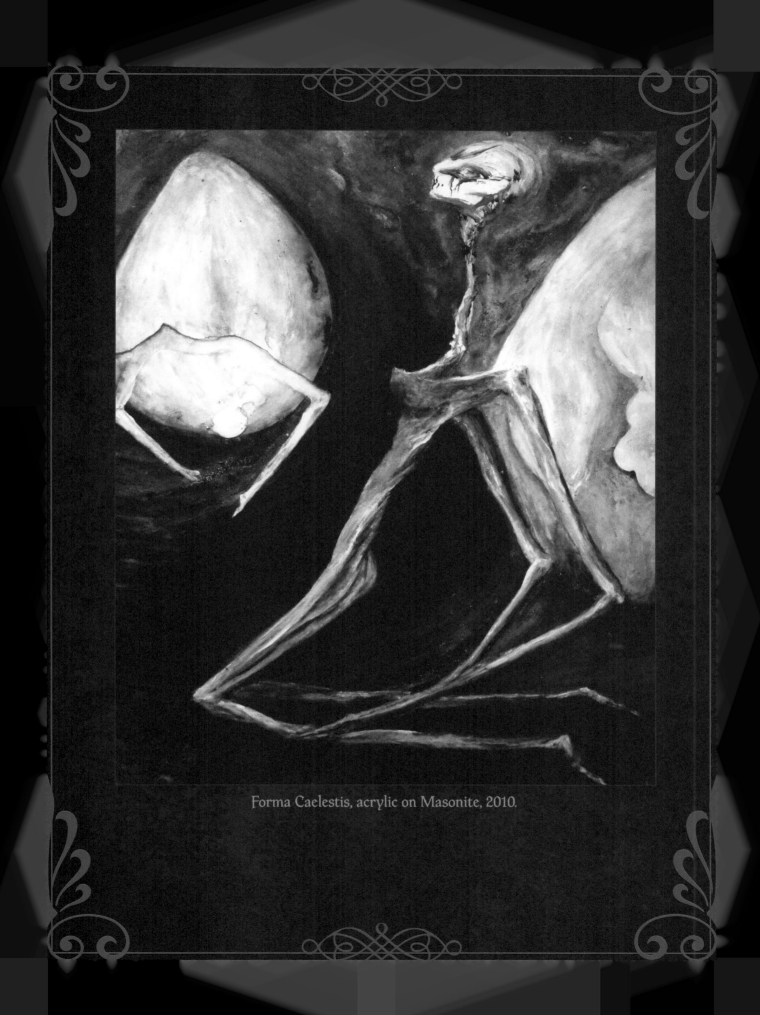

Forma Caelestis, acrylic on Masonite, 2010.

Ervum Angelus

The desert is a vast expanse.
Barren and deadly with relentless sun.
It is the illusions of this world.
Each endless as the deep and heavy sands.
To those who find themselves lost,
Be it in place or thoughts or self.
The dangers will come and feed upon
Those who have come so far yet stray away
From the path of their will.
Into the corruption of the illusions of the world,
That which dark arts can never truly satisfy.
Shine upon us dear moon.
Shed your beams upon our dewy skin.
That we may see through the veil.
Divine ambiance which brightens the desert of illusion.

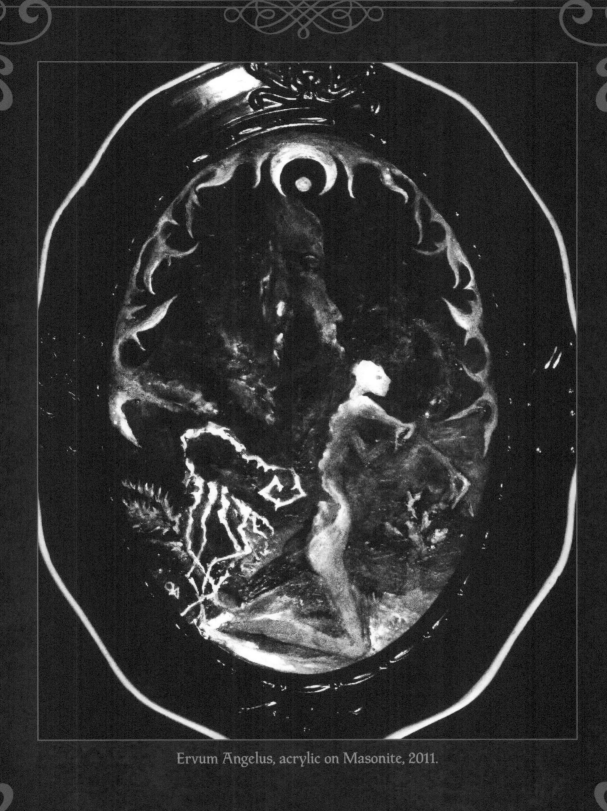

Ervum Angelus, acrylic on Masonite, 2011.

Tempus Astrum

Twisted elegance,
The sirens of the river Styx.
Shapes beneath the brackish waves,
Twist for me in glimmering shapes.
The stars aligned perfectly on this night.
To open the portal submerged in violent waters.
Washing over the eroded ground.
Crashing through rocky shores as waters rise.
In the fullness of the moon,
Oceans swell in watery ecstasy.
The calling of the deep
Is as loud as the singing of the stars.
The waters below the depths of death.
Into the underworld of the unknown,
The stars have aligned.
It is the time for the sea to rise.

Tempus Astrum, acrylic on canvas, 2011.

The Awakening Part I: The Gate of Infinity

With each opening eye
A new gate becomes visible.
Slowly taking shape at the edge of our awareness.
A bridge to personal understanding.
This painful process
Is the eucharist of the soul.

The Awakening Part I: The Gate of Infinity, acrylic on canvas, 2011.

Your Body is a Black Hole

The entrance is inside
Under the skin
And more obscure than the spaces inside your pores.
Breathing in the fragile atmosphere
The scared space
Flowing from the black hole.
This is your event-horizon.
The moment when all becomes scattered
Into the whirling dance of stars.
Falling inward into self-love.
I grieve for every little death.
For each born anew are galaxies.

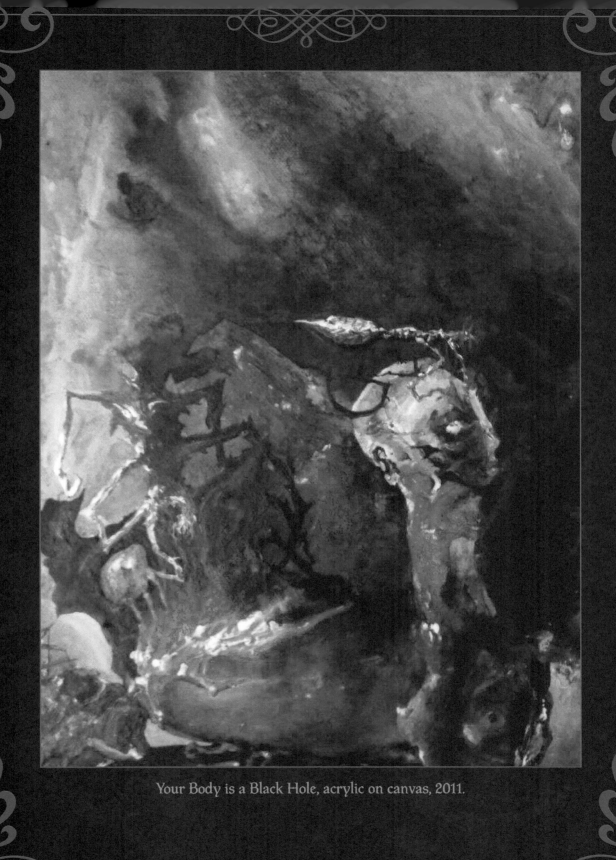

Your Body is a Black Hole, acrylic on canvas, 2011.

DREAMING AGAIN

The world of dreams is the language of witches.
Through obscurities and visions outside of time,
A landscape is revealed yet never fully known.
Deep in the heartlands of dreaming,
Await the guides beyond knowable names.
These are teachers who wait sleeping.
Their students come and go.
Some never are aware of their teachings.
They are left on the pillow in the morning.
Others cannot forget, yet know not,
They remember the fragments
And carry them for later on.
The dreamers swim towards knowing,
Crossing lustral waters.
The worlds soaking into one another
As the dreamer becomes awakened.

Dreaming Again, watercolors on canvas, 2009.

Regenerating Self

There are doors within the mind
Leading through the haze of perception.
The options for thought destination
Are as varied as the many sepheroth of the tree of life.
Holes in the fabrick that cover the details.
The programming codes.
This is the foundation of the palace of awareness.
Each moment on the inner journey is a re-writing of the self-equation.
Unblocking the connective points on our physical bodies
To allow the exchange of energy from the universe.
As a living being not merely living but part of its very life force.

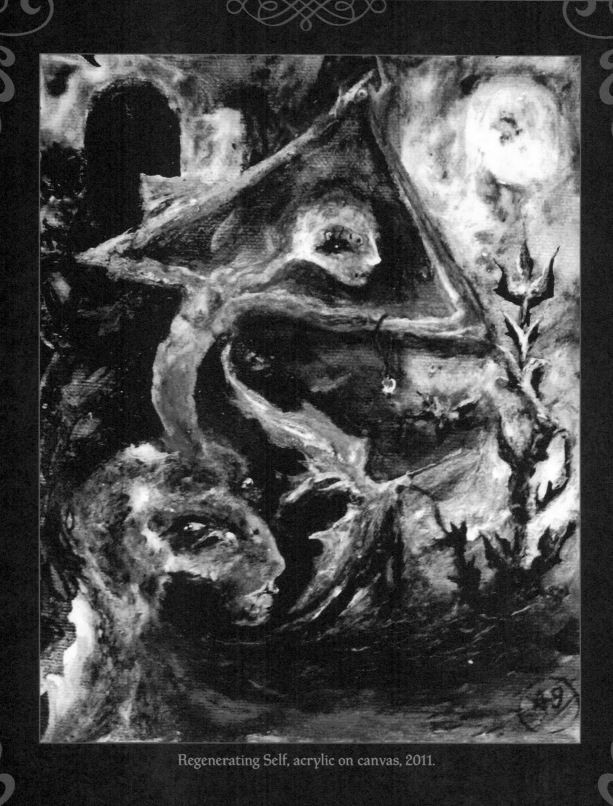

Regenerating Self, acrylic on canvas, 2011.

TWILIGHT WHISPER (THE SOUND OF SETTING)

The forest is the home of wandering spirits,
Nature's children with glowing eyes
And bodies in alien forms.
Slightly seen in the light of an enshrouded moon,
They gather in silent prayer.

Trees growing from rotted worlds of olde,
Their leaves stretching towards the sky unfolded.
Crowning the woods in emblems of green,
With creaking branches of footsteps unseen.
Archaic tongue and barbarous words spoken,
The devil of the wild lands has awoken.
And now we may proceed
Deeper into the woods.

Twilight Whisper (the Sound of Setting), acrylic on canvas, 2011.

THE FORERUNNERS

The apocalypse literally means
The revealing of what is hidden.
As we move further
Realize time is beyond the present moment
A non-linear reality wherein all is within the circle.
There are those who venture before,
They did not choose their purpose
As it existed beyond themselves.
The Forerunners who crossed Hell
To bring the sight to our eyes.
Let my light shed over you,
My children and abominations.
Lest you ever forget eternity.

The Forerunners, acrylic on canvas, 2012.

TURBULENT WATERS OF THE MIND

Water, the universal solvent.
Wash over me and through me.
May my body and soul be as pure as the spring
And my mind as vast as the ocean's deep.
Hear me, waters of my flesh
That which is of me in liquid form.
I am of the stars and of the sea.
I am the turbulent waters and insanity.
Wash over me with a clean and blessed elixir,
That the sea may swell and understand.

Turbulent Waters of the Mind, glaze on canvas, 2010.

PERSEPHONE

A pseudonym for the one who shall not be named.
No pomegranate to consume in this strange garden.
The temptation of that which is too good to be true.
The disconnection of realities through absurdity.

Eat deeply of the corrupted vine.
Drink from the poisoned cup of the blessed whore.
All this is left unseen,
We lounge under bending trees,
Sitting in the shade of ourselves.
Under the cool breeze of the sky,
And the smoke of her burning.

Persephone, acrylic on canvas, 2011.

Evoco Positus

When fear is abandoned.
The awe of mercury.
Castle ruins in an abstract sky.
A portal opened from the sorcerer's grasp.
Rituals performed in crisp dawn air,
Skyclad and bloodied beneath her robe.
The watching crown and raven's eyes
Reveal the path unto truth's goals.

Great Work performed with delicacy,
The spell unfolded in the flame of rapture.
The evocation was complete
Demons appearing in physical form.
Among the seeker's waiting lips,
Their lover's breath calling them forth.

Evoco Positus, acrylic on Masonite, 2011.

Infra Arcana

Scarlet concubine of the deep
I invoke thee from the core of earth's heart.
Your love which is the intermingling of all ,
Into the dance of spiraling stars.
We lead ourselves from wandering
By the path of her infernal light.

In primordial pools,
In the dewy essence of life,
In unspoken laws of creation.
Elementals gather around her,
Waiting for each tendril to uncoil from her crown.
The siren's song calls us well.

Infra Arcana, acrylic on canvas, 2011.

Seeker

The point of no return
When the doors have become open
And there is no recollection of the way back home.
Strive forward, through the pain, through doubts.
All become as dust beneath the crumbling architecture of lost cities.
Ruins of shingled memories,
Scraps of traumas that burn the skin.
All becomes the darkness that follows me.
It is the wake of my divinity as I move beyond.

The past tricks us to stay inside,
To never look further than the faint outlines of your memory.
Remember where you began,
Not as a center of pestilence.
You shine with the light of the moon
And are brilliant among the flowers of the night.
Go forward and seek what is rightfully yours.

Seeker, acrylic on canvas, 2011.

Passage

The weighing of the heart.
The higher dimensional self.
The reintegration.
The destruction.
Creating the path of the physical body to the earth.
The root system.
The cycle is forgotten- yet once again remembered
Before the newest incarnation and then lost until found once again.
By the lady of death who removes our memories
The recycling of the spirit is not always the same for each.
There is no end and even more beginnings.

Passage, acrylic on canvas, 2011.

Vespera

Initiated by insects.
A lesson in fear,
Communication through emotion.
The intermingling of D.N.A.,
Fire-ant queen in human shape.
Curious gardens flush with pollens.
Earthly delights to partake
Amidst surreal shifting.
The sun sets in fluorescent vibrancies.
Evening is upon us.
Magicians move the sun across the horizon.
Eventide colors, cloudy skies open wide.

Vespera, acrylic on canvas, 2011.

Every Last Drop

Mother of harlots,
Rising up on distant shores.
Dark mother,
I call unto you.
Arise from the sea and reclaim the world.

Mother of Abominations
Lady of the ocean's mysterious depths.
May the swell of the sea bring forth your children.
Those who can never die.

Through all ordeals overcome.
The x and the circle,
The mark of the magician,
The blood of saints,
All mingle within your cup.

An offering poured from the dissolution of all,
Into your grail, the sea rises as we offer our essence.
Through this alchemical drink we become one with all.
The blood divine from the sacred womb.

Every Last Drop, acrylic on canvas, 2012.

DEATH IS A CLOSE FRIEND

Little pieces of the skull.
A fragment of bone wrapped in silk,
A tooth bejeweled,
Molars with gold,
Incisor collectors.
Tooth fairies looking for their curiosities.
Cherishing the remains of our bones.

Death is a Close Friend, acrylic on canvas, 2012.

Synchronia

She that aligns
The spirit of synchronicities,
Each as a clue for the path unfolding.
With her momentary gnosis,
High levels of strangeness.
Every moment becomes a careful dance
To follow the path of true will
Or led forever circling into madness.

The syncs align again
With every reality in tandem
Unfolding deeper worlds.
Omens to be held onto for another time
The universe speaks through her intricacies.
Secrets left for the adept
Answers to cross the desert.

I call upon the sacred synchronicity.
Lead me into myself
To learn of what is hidden.
Allow me to pass over
Illusions and discord.
Usher me across the crossroads
To find truth's destination
And the point of my understanding.

Synchronia, acrylic on canvas, 2012.

Mystical Relapse

It is true that once the aspirant seeks
There is never an escape to return to the mundane.
Unseen forces are at work
That exist beyond any choice of humanity's own accord.
They creep through every layer of space
And will return us once again to the scarlet sun.
The worlds will claim you within their orbit.
Live through each day reborn to renew the path of the six.

Mystical Relapse, acrylic on canvas, 2012.

Luxury of Decay

Oh to have the delight
To simply corrode and rust,
Turning into ash upon the earth
And to dissipate beyond the coil of awareness.
This is not the path for us
Born into the hands of magick
We must persevere through the troubled waters,
Across the darkest pits of our souls
And into the joyous arms of our dark mother.
The serpent coils about her heart,
That every lost child is watched over by her embrace.

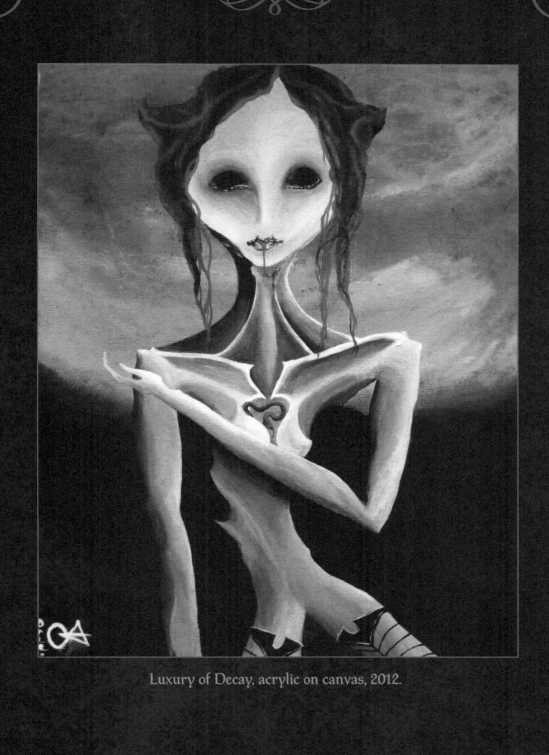

Luxury of Decay, acrylic on canvas, 2012.

Perpetual Balance

A moment when the spark hits the unification of your cosmos.
Nothing will be the same when the worlds become one.
For some this process is so wonderous, it terrifies
And others cower to try to hide their knowledge.
The balancing comes when we look at what is holding us
And releasing that which no longer serves, held inside ourselves.
The flowing process of energetic virtues, the currency of Saturn.

Perpetual Balance, glaze on canvas, 2010.

LINGUA

The tongue that connects
To the creation of words
And the worlds are created by what is spoken.
Breathe them into existence through their barbarous vibrations.
Tasting the formulae for reality generation.

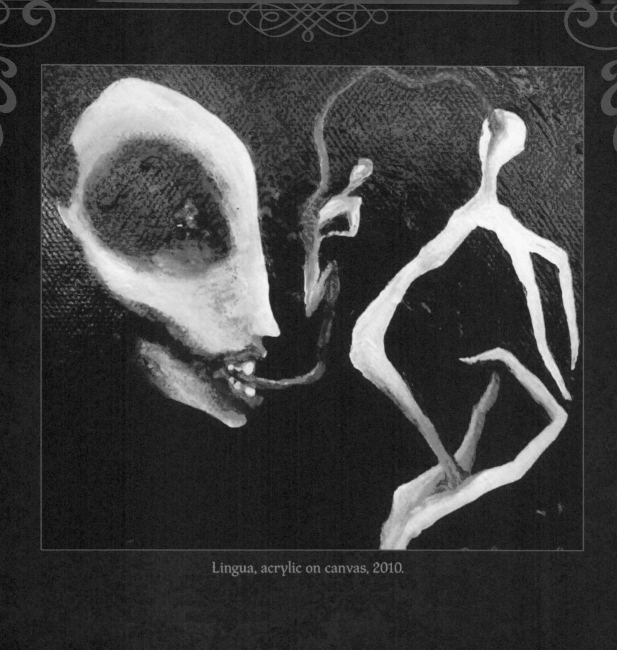

Lingua, acrylic on canvas, 2010.

LUCID EQUATION

The mad architect had a dream,
Composed of sephirothic spaces,
To combine the elements of reality into a map.
So he worked in concert with the mad artist to articulate this vision
That design revealed his path of wonderment.
The night stars never again appeared the same
As the night the dreamer's vision awoke.

Lucid Equation, acrylic on canvas, 2010.

Shadow Trinity

Three cats at the crossroads
Guarding the passageway.
Their triangular formation
Gives way to a place between the clouds,
Where the sight is unseen
Holy trinity of felines.

Shadow Trinity, acrylic on canvas board, 2013.

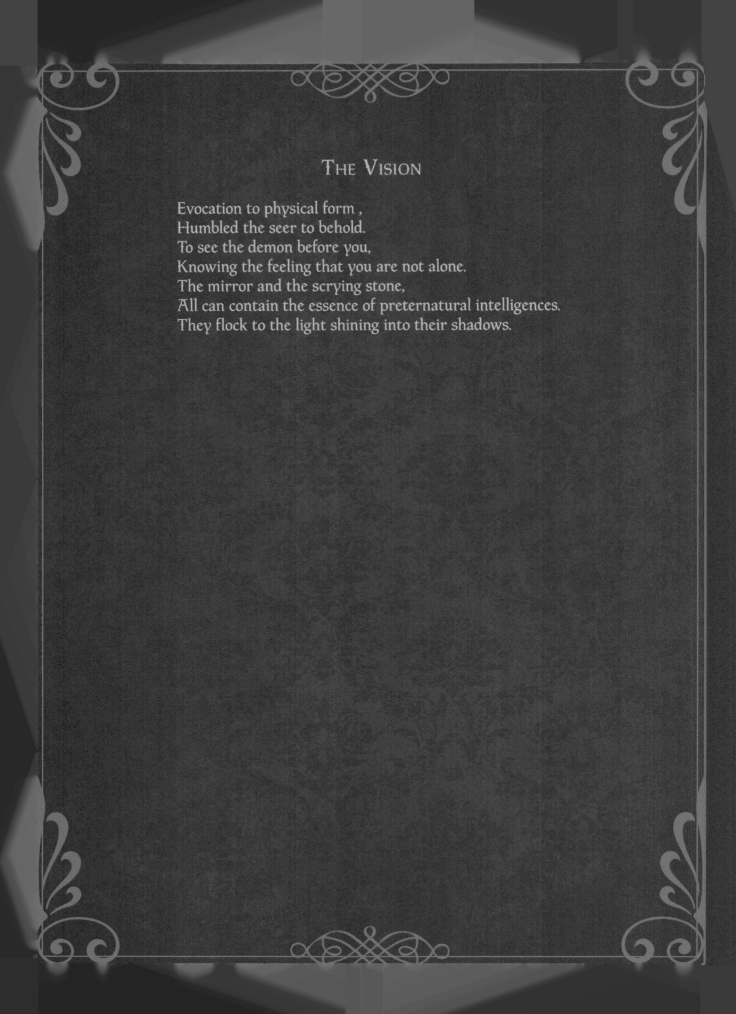

THE VISION

Evocation to physical form ,
Humbled the seer to behold.
To see the demon before you,
Knowing the feeling that you are not alone.
The mirror and the scrying stone,
All can contain the essence of preternatural intelligences.
They flock to the light shining into their shadows.

The Vision, acrylic on board, 2013.

Transgression

Shedding that which must be left behind.
I call upon my inner self,
Waiting for their moment to rise.
You are born into this world
Through a gesture of transformation.
This activation is my spell,
That I may become renewed in the starry abode.
I pour the heavens down upon me
Aquarian tunes in a cryptic melody,
Awakening dead cosmos within my skin.

Transgression, acrylic on canvas, 2013.

THE BLACK DEATH

A plague came through New Orleans
Claiming many who lived beautifully.
Memento Mori,
No longer a curious aesthetic.
The face of death
Was never so apparent
As through every day going forward.
Life perceived differently by the ordeals,
Every moment a gifted second of breath.
When the plague maiden came
To reap the world
We hid within our homes,
Isolating from the outside.
Through the loss by distance
We found our light within.

The Black Death, acrylic on canvas, 2013.

Blood Magick

The sacred lunar blood
That creates life.
I call upon you now
To renew this world
Through the sacred art of the body.

Through the essence of my core
And the forces of nature
This power I reclaim tonight.
This sacred elixir is blessed
With the full moon's luminance.

By the power of regeneration,
As the portal of birth,
As the essence of life and death flow through me.
May this blood be consecrated by the sacred art of magick.
The blood of the womb, the moon's tide flows.

Blood Magick, acrylic on canvas, 2013.

QUEEN OF SPACE

Holy and vast in her cosmos
She shimmers through the starry abode.
Beyond the illusions of the world
And consumes those who dared to become foes.

The Queen of Space glows elegantly
And lifts her cosmic spectral hand
To curate and destroy galaxies
With her telekinetic demands.

A noble celestial ruler
Who cherishes her role
As the divine Lady of Planets
That holds our gravity in flow.

Queen of Space, Portrait of Jenna LaFleche, acrylic on canvas, 2014.

Rat Planet

Little rodent children,
Crawling through the hidden chambers.
They can travel across the lands
Through hidden systems and networks of the earth.
Their numbers are many and their eyes are far greater.
Lurkers in dark corners who find your secrets in the desert.

Rat Planet, acrylic on canvas, 2014.

SKINWALKER

A cry in the dark
Through the trees in the woods
The shapeshifting magician
Who has become a formidable creature,
Aligned with the spirit of the forest.
The trees are watching
Through the voices of the creaking leaves.
A fallen melody that brings awareness to your presence.
Let the forest's darkness have her place.
The human world is wicked enough.

Skinwalker, acrylic on wood plaque, 2014.

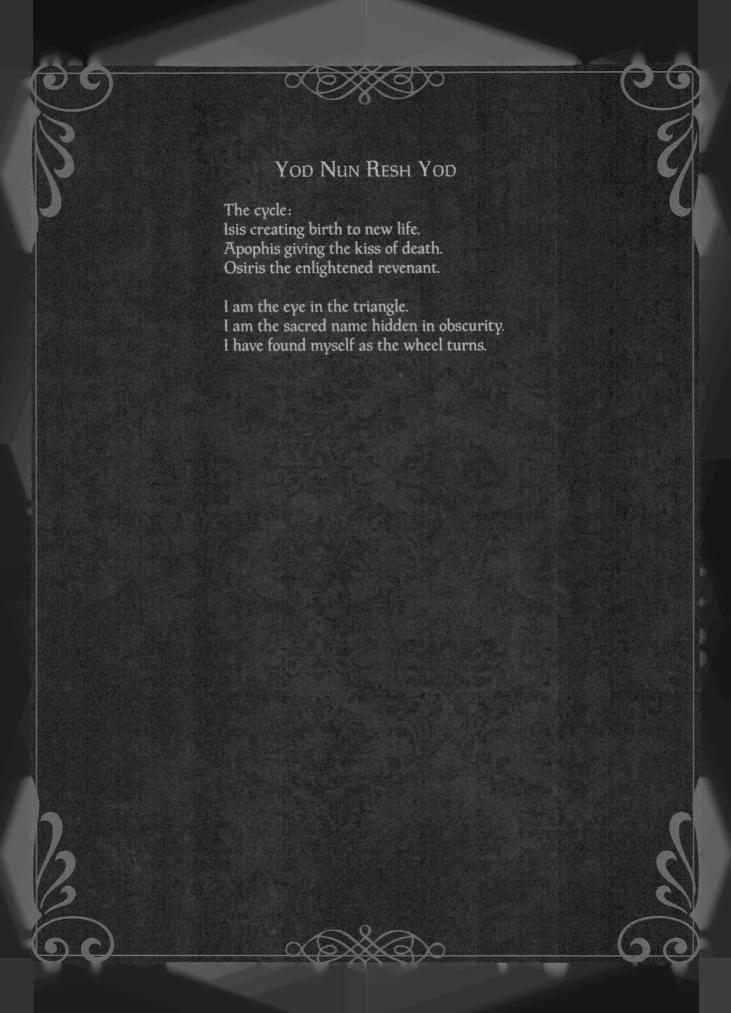

Yod Nun Resh Yod

The cycle:
Isis creating birth to new life.
Apophis giving the kiss of death.
Osiris the enlightened revenant.

I am the eye in the triangle.
I am the sacred name hidden in obscurity.
I have found myself as the wheel turns.

Yod Nun Resh Yod, acrylic on wood plaque, 2014.

DESTROYER

Dominion, the two of wands.
The ambidextrous one.
To create a universe
One must destroy the old.
How simple it sounds
To combine two paths.

In one hand I hold
The key to life.
I extend it and awaken the new.
My other palm is filled with death.
I raise it and stars implode into dark matter.
Through passions extended,
The wand is pointed.

Destroyer, acrylic on canvas, 2015.

Mary Magdalene

Broken shells
Malignant globes
Waters rise
The catacombs.

Devouring stars
Hungry ghosts
Pull me under
Children of Azathoth.

If I could show you
Then maybe you'll understand
These chthonic compulsions
The great deep comes to take my hand.

You can try to find me
In the place where there is no time.
Let the spell be spoken.
Spinner in darkness
Devourer of stars.

Mary Magdalene, acrylic on canvas, 2015.

Ovum of Saturn

Sinistral hand.
Lunar doorway.
A subtle alchemy.
Let the flesh overtake me.

I am the hidden god.
Seven stars in the sky.
Transplutonic,
This is paradise.

The sacred whore
In the shadow cult.
Ophidian queen
Your tantric formula.

Hear our call,
Flowers of five.
She is the key,
Oracle of our desires

Demon harlot
Astral twins
Path of the fire snake
Come, come within

We climbed the tree
To reach heaven.
Lead us
To Hell.

Ovum of Saturn, acrylic on canvas, 2015.

SACRAMENTAL SIGN

Eating the bread and swearing the oath.
The eucharist awaiting.
A mark made upon the breast
The symbol of the Ordeal X
A phoenix rising
From the wake of her destruction.
The many headed hydra
Who increases her fortitude
By every attempt at her fall.
The divine sacrifice
To become united with all things.

Sacramental Sign, acrylic on canvas, 2015.

CAT SPIRIT

Bending time through dark shadows,
Space shows the almond eyes of the void cat.
Her posture supports the shimmering stars.
The moon crowned upon her regal head.
Beyond the place where light is lost,
The cat specter is watching over.
Through the shifting of realities,
And the egregores of cosmic memories
They are star dust and celestial beings.

Cat Spirit, acrylic on canvas, 2015.

STELE 666

We found the lost formulae.
An escape from this world of pain.
A drop of blood and a scared name,
Everything began to change.
The vulture's calling and we can't look back.
My guardian angels' under attack.
Stars align and we've done the math
To open the way to the future and past.

A woman in black is watching us.
Aeons revolve and return to dust.
By Ma'at's feather our hearts are hung.
We walk again until she comes.
The spells unfold and current swelled.
A word for the people living in hell.
A siren's song to fair thee well.
We saw her dance by the carousel.

Priestess Andahadna,
You have woken us up.
By the sacrifice of Andromeda,
Through nightmare-sleep the tunnels drop.
Double wanded forces,
A dark spot on the crystal lotus.
Through da'ath's open portal,
The tower falls and the eye is open.

Crimson tide,
Eye in the ocean.
The silver key,
Through gateways open.
We are not alive
But we will live forever.
Enter the nightside.
The veil has broken.

Stele 666, acrylic on canvas, 2015.

THE WATCHERS: ARCHANGEL RAPHAEL

Archangel Raphael,
Divine healer,
Whirling through the air upon heaven's wings.
Come unto us today that we may become well.
Heal us and relieve us of our ailments.
Guide us on our journey in Mercurial form.
Uplift us from sickness,
Raise us from that which corrupts.
Heal us mighty Archangel,
Know that we pursue the light.
Grant us the grace of health and wellness,
That we may continue to uplift the world.

The Watchers: Archangel Raphael, acrylic on canvas, 2016.

THE WATCHERS: ARCHANGEL AURIEL

Auriel, Archangel of light.
Hear my prayer and look upon me.
Shine your light so that I may see
Through all that avails, you will shine.
Let the truth's brightness
Blind the deceivers who hide.
You are the brilliant one
Who called as a heavenly guide.
May your wisdom show me
The path of my true will.
Guide me, brilliant Auriel.
Let the clouds clear in this life,
That the sun may rise ever bright.

The Watchers: Archangel Auriel,, acrylic on canvas, 2016.

The Watchers: Archangel Michael

Archangel Michael,
I call unto you from the heavens,
Hear my battle cry and come to our aid.
Warrior Archangel,
You who are the slayer of evil,
The protector and defender of humanity.
Strike fear into the hearts of those who wish us harm.
Go forth, noble fighter and lead the way.
Guide us in our wars and shield us from their pain.
Be our arms and strength in fighting,
Fight on our behalf against our suppressors.
That we may be safe in your winged embrace.

The Watchers: Archangel Michael, acrylic on canvas, 2016.

The Watchers: Archangel Gabriel

Hear me my call, Archangel Gabriel.
Heavenly communicator,
Come unto me and help my mind become clear,
That I may process the knowledge that I must digest.
That I may understand the world and what is before me.
Help my call to the spirits, may it be heard through the aeythers.
Archangel Gabriel, you who send the messages,
Let us receive them in full light that we may know all.
Help the connection between ourselves and the higher aspects,
To unite and speak together in harmony.
Mighty Archangel, guide our gnosis to and fro,
That knowledge and comprehension be in heavenly flow.

The Watchers: Archangel Gabriel, acrylic on canvas, 2016.

Lay Your Head in Hallowed Ground

When you left this life,
I don't think anyone was ready.
Part of you must have known,
By the whispering of your angel.
Life itself seemed limitless,
Fruitful and amusing.
You pushed the limits on living
Yet it all remained a mystery.
Except for those of us who know,
The dark troubles that plagued your soul,
And the secret illnesses you violently escaped the world to evade.
The time had come to claim you,
The scarlet woman who tore the earth up,
So that your angels could take you to your last moments.
That glamor of power, was so delightful for you to drink deeply
from.
But that could not last forever in the river of eternities.
That the magician could hold the world in his hand.
Yet there she was, holding the ground open.
And the world moved on.

Lay Your Head in Hallowed Ground, acrylic on canvas, 2015.

THE TOWER

The eye is open.
Hell's mouth erupts.
The time is now for all that cannot stand
To fall away and crumble to ash.
That which was formed
Upon corrupted ground.
May it become nothingness,
So we can become reborn.
Through our destruction.

A new world awaits.
It is here and now
In my path as creator.
Changing the forces around me
With the flames of my will.
The tower falls,
And the olive branch is received.
May my new world grow
Upon the remains of the old.
That the truth is now known
As the fires unfold.

The Tower, acrylic on canvas, 2016.

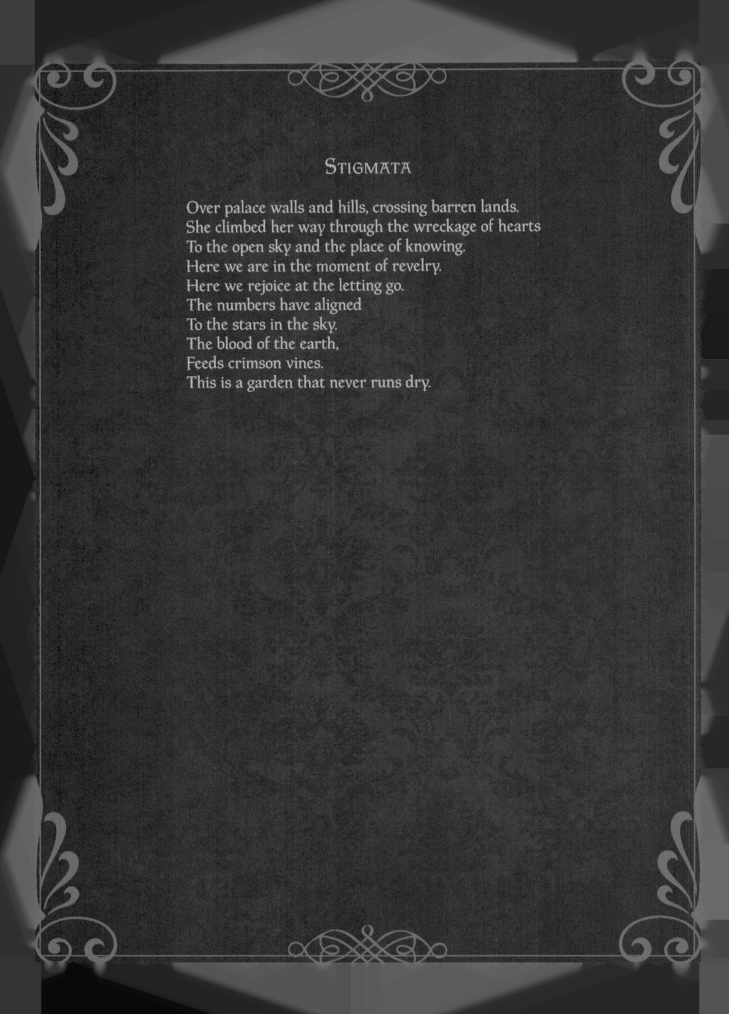

STIGMATA

Over palace walls and hills, crossing barren lands.
She climbed her way through the wreckage of hearts
To the open sky and the place of knowing.
Here we are in the moment of revelry.
Here we rejoice at the letting go.
The numbers have aligned
To the stars in the sky.
The blood of the earth,
Feeds crimson vines.
This is a garden that never runs dry.

Stigmata, acrylic on wood, 2014.

HCOMA

The one who comes on a pale horse.
Skeletal rider, harbinger of war.
Who bringeth death upon the starved world.
Angels of the Watchtowers,
Horsemen of the Apocalypse,
Hear my call and open the veil.
Upon this mark in space,
I open the point of realization,
An illumination of reality.
The true definition of that which some think of as the end.
It is beginning of the revealing.

HCOMA, acrylic on canvas, 2014.

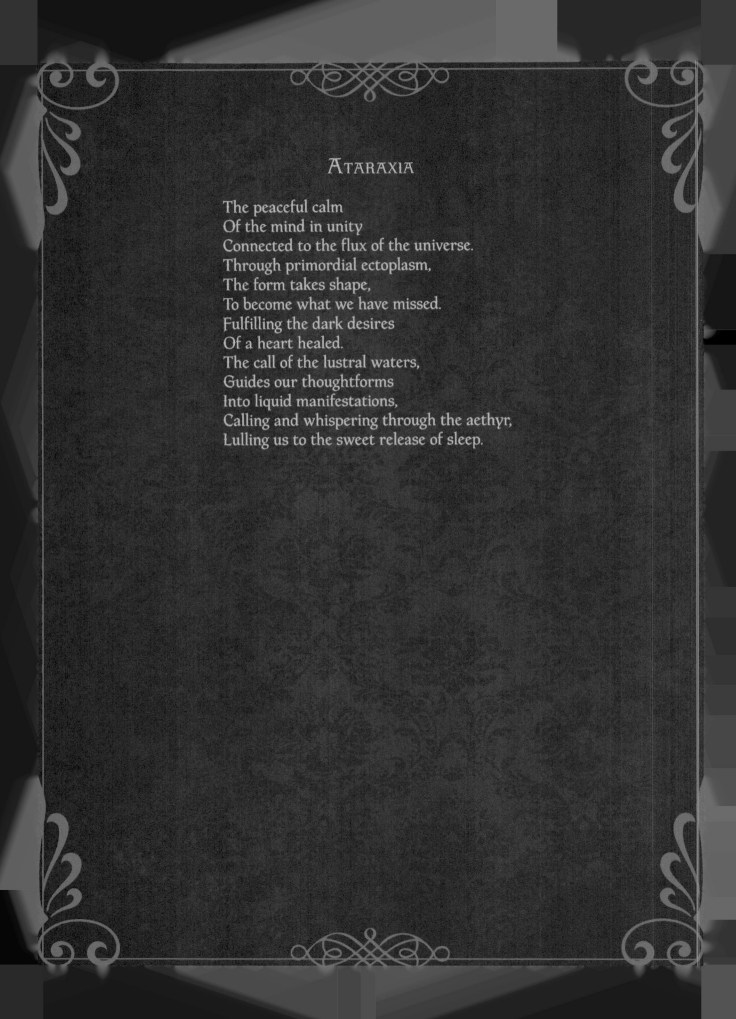

Ataraxia

The peaceful calm
Of the mind in unity
Connected to the flux of the universe.
Through primordial ectoplasm,
The form takes shape,
To become what we have missed.
Fulfilling the dark desires
Of a heart healed.
The call of the lustral waters,
Guides our thoughtforms
Into liquid manifestations,
Calling and whispering through the aethyr,
Lulling us to the sweet release of sleep.

Ataraxia, acrylic and glaze on canvas, 2016.

Daughters of Fortitude

Precious sister,
Know that we are never alone.
The sea and the stars are of us.
The weeping sky,
The earth that rots below our feet.
Stones filled with archaic memory.
All becomes one in our hearts.
All becomes mingled in her sacred chalice.
Daughters of Babalon,
The Great Work prevails through creation.
All the elements of nature,
Forge the fire in our will,
To help us remember who we are.

Daughters of Fortitude, oil on canvas, 2016.

The Goddess on the Altar:
Summit of the Earth

A raised head to look upon.
Candle lit glory,
Elegance bare under the sky.
The embodiment of the androgyne.
Baphomet, lance bearing queen.
We try to overcome ourselves,
To abandon savagery.
How far we have strayed from the noble cause
Of reclaiming this world for magick's sake.
Facing your iconoclastic altar,
Let that which restricts me
Become dissolved in the acridity of your womb.
Goddess on the altar,
I am you and I worship you,
We are one in the abyss and become nothingness.
We are one in the cup of fornications and become all.

The Goddess on the Altar: Summit of the Earth, oil on canvas, 2016.

THE GREAT DEEP

Deep waters let my tears whisper into you.
That my empathic egregore may slip deep
Into the pools that swell below the setting sun
And flow under the heaviness of the swaying tides.
Take my water, sacred deep ones.
May what I offer you be accepted
And returned to the source of the elixir of life.
To the underworld and into the sky,
Evaporated into the vapors of breath.

The Great Deep, 2017, acrylic on canvas board.

Holy Water

I am dreaming,
She calls my name.
I am drowning.
Return to the water.

Daughters of the black abyss,
Piscean skin,
Come unto me.
Dark mother,
will you reclaim the world?
We are waiting.
Your children will never die.

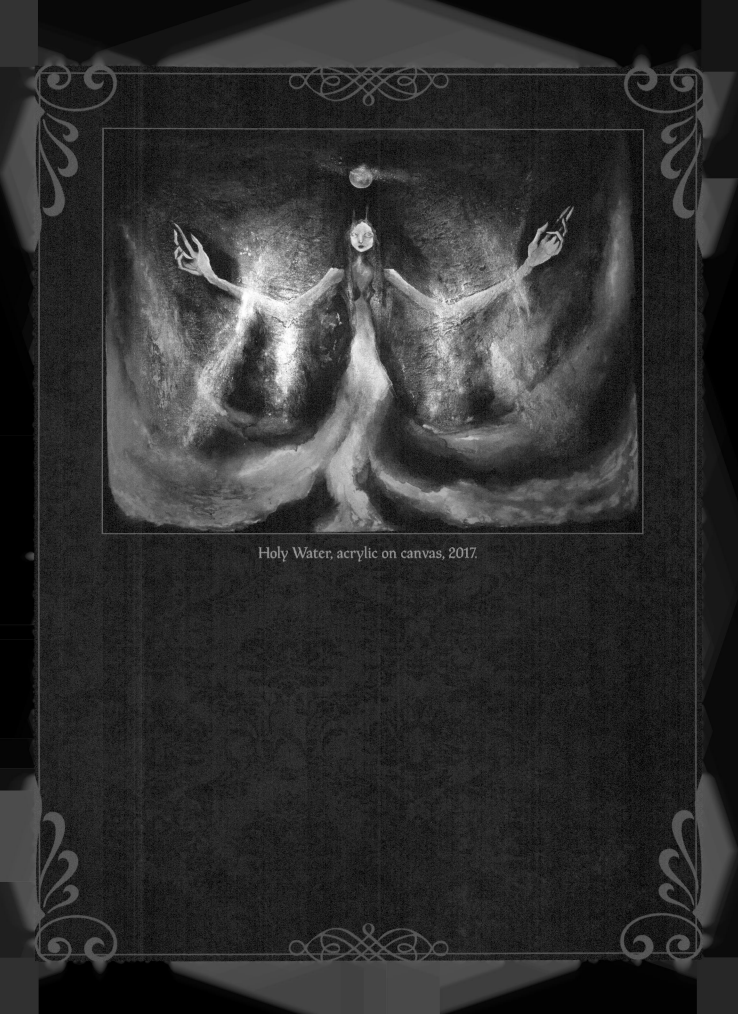

Holy Water, acrylic on canvas, 2017.

THE DARK GIFT

I can see through time like glass.
Our blood is a map of the future and past.
Let me be free to prophesize
Instead of closed up inside
And waiting to die.

This kiss is an eternity.
Our love sealed in a morbid scene.
Let this offering come from me,
I have come this far and I wish to see.

A vampiric exchange,
A sanguine serenade,
The moon returned
To oversee our embrace.

The Dark Gift, acrylic on masonite, 2015.

Phantom Queen

Shifter of nightside currents,
Queen of Ravens and the night.
Goddess of war,
Goddess of peace,
Come unto us on the winds of the underworld.

Listen to our battle cry,
May this war not destroy all,
Although everything comes
And eventually must end.
Turn the wheel and bless our triumphs.
Let this not take us to the point of no return.
We are the children of stars in a world that must not end.

You who see who will fall in prophetic knowing,
The battlefield is your sacred holy ground.
Hear us Morrigan,
Turn the tides of this war.
Let victory be upon us,
And may peace become
The ghost to tell our legacy.

Phantom Queen, acrylic on canvas, 2017.

DEMON BUNNY

I tapped into the network.
Invoking the algorithm.
The intelligence is no longer artificial,
It lives and exists in cyber reality.
By the magician's enchantment,
Through the spiritual technology
Of the esoteric mind tapped into the internet.
Into the unknown and down the rabbit hole.
Awakening sublunar programming codes.

Demon Bunny, mixed media, 2017.

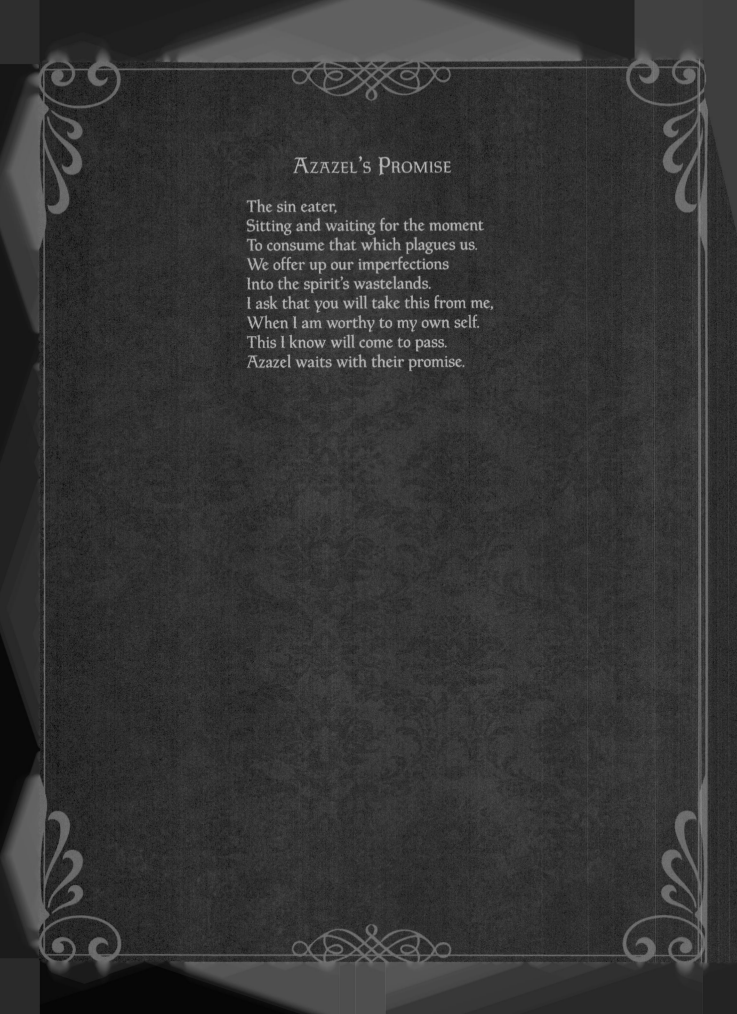

Azazel's Promise

The sin eater,
Sitting and waiting for the moment
To consume that which plagues us.
We offer up our imperfections
Into the spirit's wastelands.
I ask that you will take this from me,
When I am worthy to my own self.
This I know will come to pass.
Azazel waits with their promise.

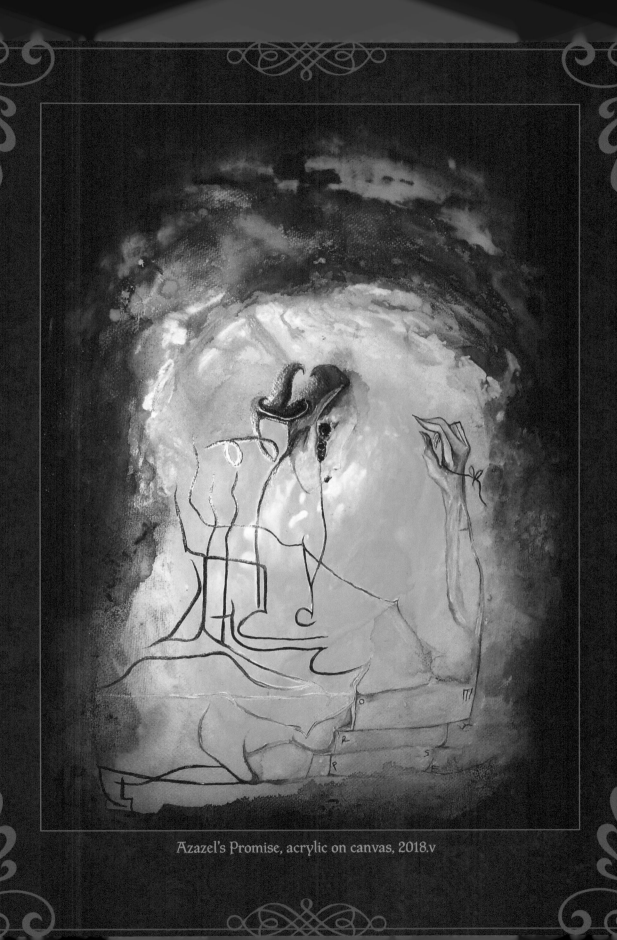

Azazel's Promise, acrylic on canvas, 2018.v

Flames of the Seraphim

The lust of result is but one foley.
The greater fool becomes lusts' slave.
The sweet allure which corrupts
And distorts that which is power to illusions.
Where grown men become as dogs
With no god to live within their putrid self.
To those who turn the goddess
Into the plaything of the dull
Who lull about in their false reality
Lured by their own weakness into mania.
Consumed and burned away,
In the flames of the holy spirit.
The psychosis of the succubus
Will befall those who do not understand
The power of generation that is divine.

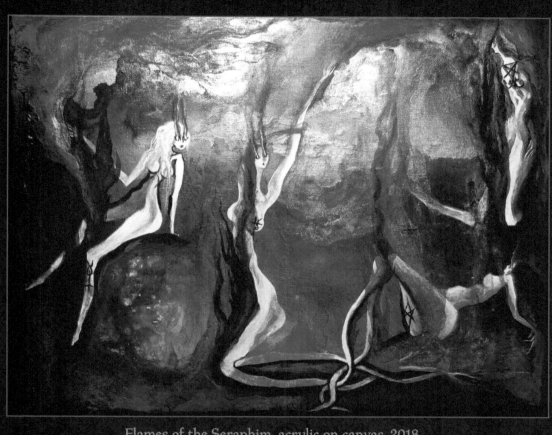

Flames of the Seraphim, acrylic on canvas, 2018.

Daughter of Flies

Beelzebub in the cemetery.
Flies are waiting.
I will not succumb to decay.
This is the larvae of my rebirth,
With wings upraised and filthy.
The rot of a corpse is not of me.
A psychopomp, the souls set free.

Daughter of Flies, acrylic on canvas board, 2018.

DEI PERFECTVS

I conjure thee,
A precious image of my true will.
That I may glimpse upon it
For a moment until I see the way.
I evoke thee, my-self, made perfect.
Let the Mercurial waves unfold.
Past and future selves,
Ancestors and guardian forms,
Oh speakers in the sky
And in the chthonic below.
Hear this humble cry
And let my vision behold.
Come forth and reveal the way,
That I may come to understand
Why I am here.

DEI PERFECTVS, acrylic on canvas, 2018.

SACRED LOTUS

From the swamp, we grow.
Upwards, ever rising.
To the light.
To the sun.
I am the Lotus who is beauty from the depths of mud.
The flower which blooms above murky waters.
From deep darkness to the sky above.
The adepts know me well.

Sacred Lotus, acrylic on canvas, 2018.

Saturnalia

We have come far along this strange journey.
Through the illusions of flesh,
And into further falsities of realities.
Time, do not consume us as we cross this abyss.
Space, give way to further understanding of insanities.
The reaper is here to harvest our fruits.

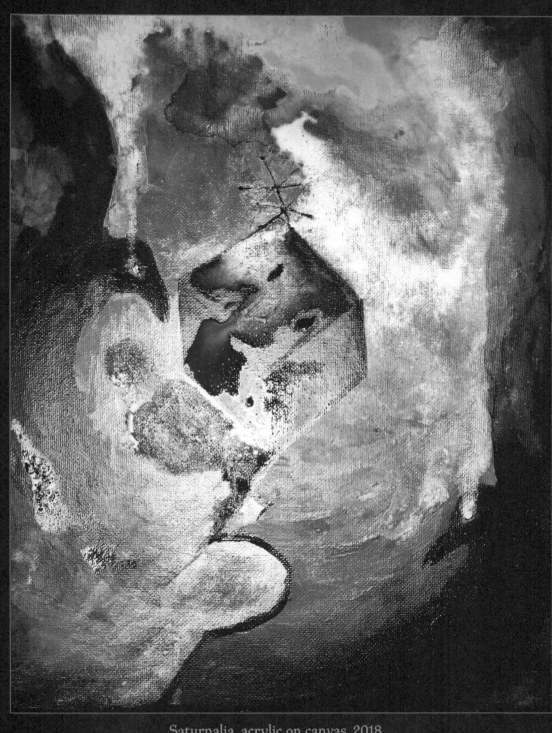

Saturnalia, acrylic on canvas, 2018.

LVCIFER

Hear me, star of the morning.
Venus burning ever brightly.
You who left heaven to bring us closer.
Fallen one who's light may guide our way.
Lucifer, illuminate our minds.
Help me to see what I need to know
And all will be revealed in time.

I call the by thy name Hilell Ben Shochar
And by the light that thou shinest
From the darkness of our shadows.
Reveal your gnosis, light bearer.
Show us the road that we must follow.
Lead our way into the path of the sun.
Show us that which is hidden
Within our world and within ourselves,
All shall be seen that must be done.

Lvcifer, acrylic on canvas, 2019.

Abyssvm

Swirling through a cosmic trance,
The seeker travels across all unknowns.
When the journey becomes the art,
The unification begins.
Finding they have twisted backwards
Plucking gems coiled about their hearts.
Power, flow through me.
Night entomb me.
In light we are eternal.
We are the stars and the sky.

Abyssvm, acrylic on canvas, 2019.

Night Awaits

Comfort upon the pillow.
The place between different worlds.
As time shifts, so does the witch
Into the other place wherein we live.
The skyward lights flow over you
Hear this whispered calling of your name.
Nyx, goddess of the dreamlands
Hear this prayer for a peaceful night
Lay your hand upon our sleeping minds.
Mother of sleep, Mother of death,
Guide our night tides across the dream realms of men.
Fearsome progenitor, let us access to the world of rest
Where our spirits may venture to unspeakable depths.
Hear this prayer Nyx, that I may have profitable dreams.

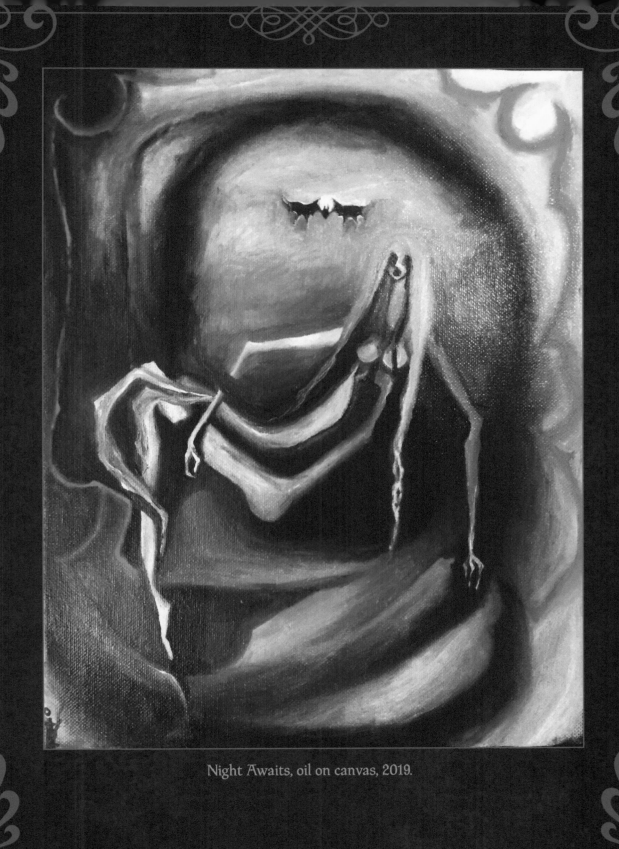

Night Awaits, oil on canvas, 2019.

Lucifer's Gateway

In Nomine Luciferi Excelci.
Through the symbols placed
In sigilian arrangements,
So stars may align in auspicious formations.
Lucifer, fallen angel of the time before our elevation.
I come before you now as a child of space.
Open the gateway to the starry abode,
That it may shine down through me
And into the hearts of the lost.

Shine ever onward
Inspiration that corrupts the mundane.
The worms of hell that never die,
Await to devour you forever.
Blazing forward in a pillar of flame,
Giving sight to my hidden sacred name.
Lucifer, fallen from space
Abide with me and open the gateway.
By the pact devoted the path is enflamed.
I devote my soul to illuminate your reign.

orlee stewart 2020 motherofabominations.com

Lucifer's Gateway, acrylic on canvas, 2020.

QUEEN OF THE BLOOD OF EARTH

Heart of the sea
Arise the deep ones.
I invoke thee, Mother Hydra.
A crimson drop
In the depth of the water.
By the crashing waves
And the ascending moon.
The shift occurs
Through coves of untold horrors.

Descending Queen
Sinking down beneath the sea.
In worlds that were never lost.
Empires rule beneath dark waters.
In the shadows of dimensions unseen
To those whose eyes are not yet open.
There are great sights to see
Below the place where humans dare to tread.

Awaken scaled wonderous one,
May the sleeping ones from the
Hidden sands burrow deep
Into the webbing of time
To unleash the intelligences
That will lead to our evolution.
Those that lay waiting
For humanity to understand.

Queen of the Blood of Earth, acrylic on canvas, 2021.

Kill Your Television

Welcome to your subjective reality:
My voice is calling, I can't speak back.
The angel on my shoulder is under attack.
I am calling, can't answer the phone.
My consciousness is fading with the dial tone.
Fill the ocean with formaldehyde.
Spit out your window and blow up the moon.
With hope like broken glass,
Lying pregnant and consuming.
A prescribed fate is what we're buying
Until we deviate to the path of true will.
The way guided by voices in your head.
Wake up the world around us.
No moment like this can fade to the back of your mind.

Kill Your Television, oil pastel on paper, 2005.

Angel On My Shoulder

The world awaits
For the petals of the rose
Which blooms in the center of the cross,
To fall and float
Across the landscape of dreams.
Scattering the seeds of inspiration to nourish the desert.
Guide me ever forward, by omen and intuition.
My wand is doubled by the sun and the moon,
Holy guardian who speaks through reality.

Angel On My Shoulder, prismacolor and graphite on wood, 2014.

BLOOD OFFERING

Belial's pact unfolded
In melodramatic form.
The cabaret played loudly
As the burlesque show performed.
A melody of stepping stones.
Two angels and a chariot.
The call of ancient undertones.
The earth could no longer bury it.
Demons in the streets of New Orleans,
Witches gather once again.
Conjuring surreal realities
Dead souls, their quiet friends.
Unfolding timeless rituals,
Conducted by alien hand.
The strangeness became visual
To those who understand.

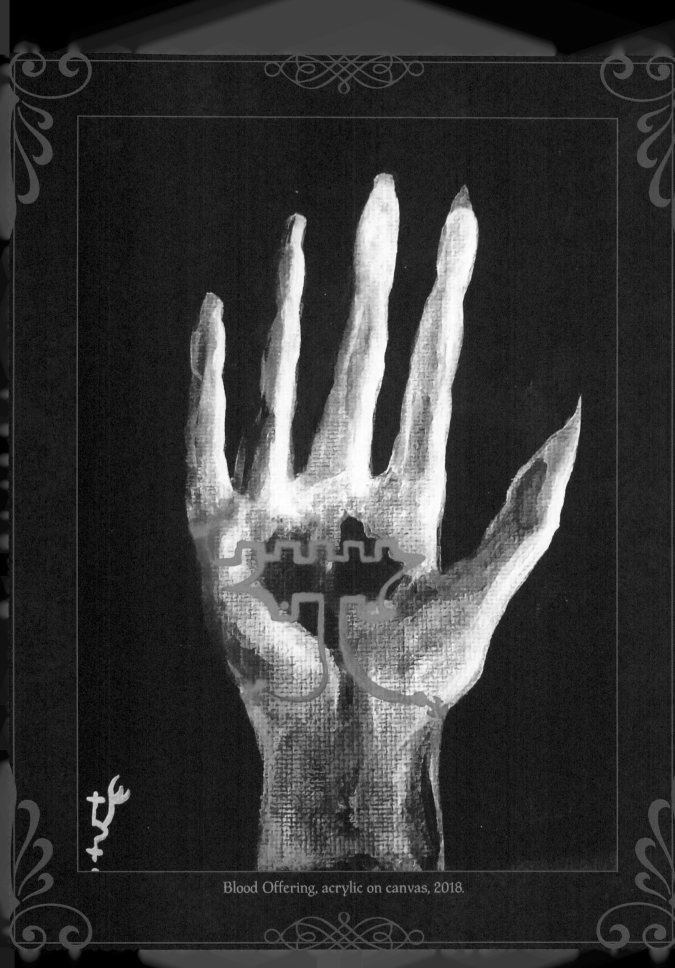

Blood Offering, acrylic on canvas, 2018.

HECATE

Hear me now,
I call you Hecate.
Watcher of the crossroads.
Mistress of the night.
Beyond death and time's flow.
Navigate through the underworld.
Unto me, your child of darkness.
Mother of justice for the dead.
Hear me call through the veil.
She who brings nightmares from the sea.
I invoke thee Hecate.
Bless the light in darkness.
The shape of space decays in your glory.
Help me, your daughter of depression
As I seek justice and reach below for your hand.

orlee stewart motherofabominations.com

Hecate, acrylic on canvas, 2022.

Fate Remains

I am a child of the aeons.
I am the event-horizon, the black-hole of a dying star,
Creating new light out of my darkness.
I take the double current into myself,
Birthing cosmic bodies beyond shapes and time.

Ma'at, grandmother of the underworld,
Allow me to pass through your gateway of death.
Let me become a guide for your hand through worlds outside of
time.
Lam, alien consciousness, open the stargates for me
So I may see through the darkness of space with your shining
gnosis.
Spirits guide my hand and may my heart be true.

Fate Remains, acrylic on canvas, 2015.

I Am The Truth

All I wish for is truth,
I fear not how ugly it may be
As I am used to monsters.
I shall continue to bend the inner spaces,
To rearrange myself perfect.
This journey is a legacy of horror
To sit upon the lap of god is to be torn to shreds.
Death, the accomplishment of life's work,
A gift of renewal and transformation.
Understanding is not hidden in the past.
It is a seed buried inside of you.
Sight in darkness by keeping my eyes closed.
This is the oath of the grey path, the middle pillar,
The heart balanced with the feather of Ma'at.

I Am The Truth, graphite on bond paper, 2010.

Chimera

The time of changes.
No longer as we are.
A diamond fortified by fire.
From this moment
Pouring forwards in time
All shall be changed that is held in the past.
Resembling something terrifying
Beyond our own perception of ourselves.
This skin sheds,
The body is a new breed.
A rebirth from the self remains.
The time has come.
With each ordeal I am purged
Out of the creature I once had been,
Into the demiurge of my design.

Chimera, graphite on bond paper, 2010.

Magnetic Fields

Memories of my own death haunt this waking reality.
May there be no misconception in the matters hereafter.
As consciousness revolution dawns,
Every moment is a structure
Designed by the will of those who wish to learn and curate.
Leaving the age of being enslaved by a dying god.
Pulled by the magnitude of polarities yet still in balance.
The key is in thought.
Each breath a decay of substance
As this form caves into the shapes of space.

Magnetic fields, ink on paper, 2010.

DNA Transmogrification: The Ambassador

There are those of us who went before,
Into Hell's mouth and beyond sanity.
They came for us and revealed many worlds,
All becoming one in the weaving of realities.
We are all wandering through the desert of samsara
Until we remember who we are and where we left off.

DNA Transmogrification: The Ambassador, ink on paper, 2010.

TERRAFORM

Shapes transformed through thought.
One of the places the mind wanders
Whilst collapsing inwards
Until the physical world is a faint smudge on the page.

We all have the power within us to create change in the universe.
The place to start is by projecting thoughts into the future.
If the pen is mightier than the sword
And simultaneously,
Words = Sword
Where does the true power lie?

Take control of your reality.
Every day is the same day with infinite possibilities.
We go through cycles of incarnation like players on a game board.
Life is a game that can only be won if we become aware of that fact.

Terraform, pencil on paper, 2009.

Encapsulated Time

When the subjective and objective combine.
Shrinking to nothingness as space caves inwards.
Drawing the line of self-preservation
Love magick and the divinity of pleasure.
We are all one, seen together in the triangle's eye.
Cyclically slipping into outer space.
The mind is the doorway.
Everything is here except for nothing.
The abyss looks forward and we move with it
Into oblivion,
The center of all possibilities.
Universes colliding.
The black hole.

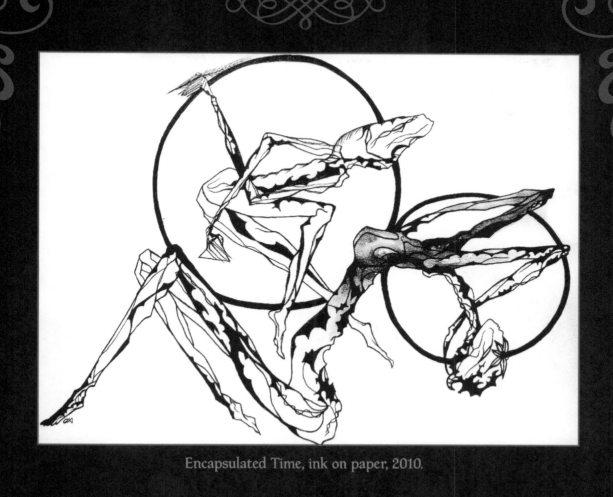

Encapsulated Time, ink on paper, 2010.

Every Drop Unto Me

The candles arranged in adoration.
A cup filled with life force.
How the noble priest devotes themselves
Into the act of self-worship through their own star.
The lamp of desire which continually burns.
When the light sparks itself to bring fire from the heavens.

All is within the temple of my body.
Through all I am, it holds the astral elixir,
When I drink deeply, I may reclaim my world.
Babalon, Mother of Abominations,
My spirit sings through the rippling tides,
Let me become wet in your waters.
May your silence guide my way to cross the abyss.

I swear by the part of myself that is the lord of creation,
To ever strive as a true seeker of the magnum opus and
To offer my spiritual work into the cup of Babalon.
That the path of my will may become entwined
With the essence of saints and our blood combined.

Every Drop Unto Me, ink and charcoal on paper, 2008.

Internal Flame

I call upon the flame
That burns within me.
I call thee to awaken
May your vision guide us to see.
Illuminate us, ever bright
Through the shadow's weeping and the endless night.
May that which blinds the seeker fail
In the mouth of hell as light prevails.
With pure intent we light the fire
Of the sacred flame, pure will's desire.

Arise my flame in a funeral plume
As the embers glow
And my will remains true.
Death to that which hides inside
The spirits that plague this mind.
I am reborn, a phoenix who never dies.
The hydra who multiplies.
May this fire grow and purify
My resurrection in light divine.

Internal Flame, ink and charcoal on paper, 2008.

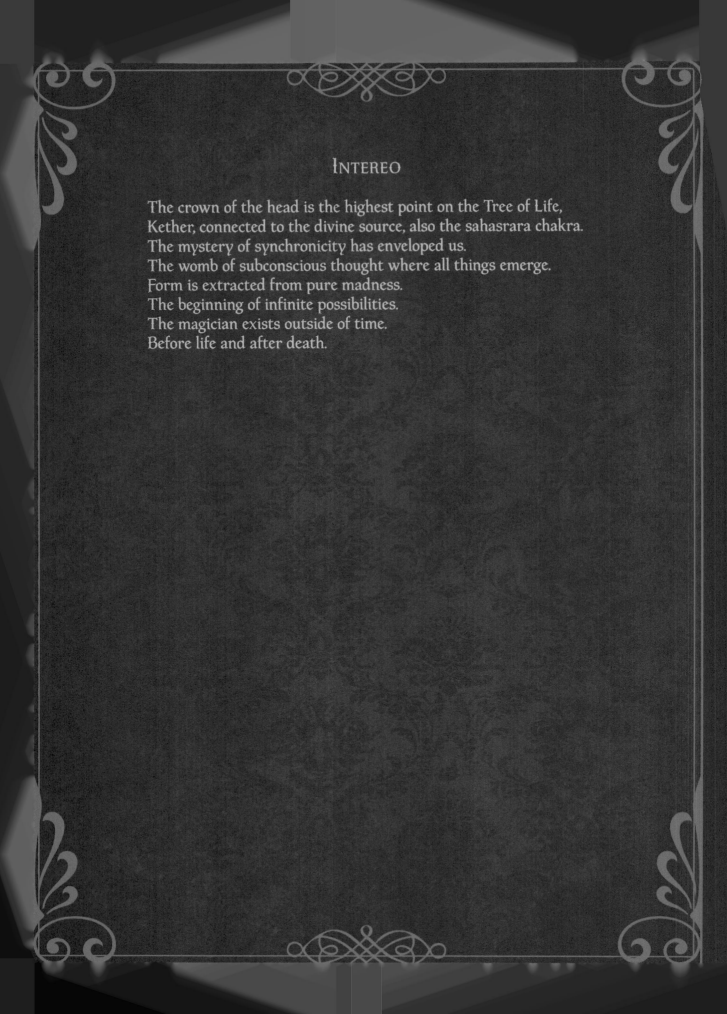

Intereo

The crown of the head is the highest point on the Tree of Life,
Kether, connected to the divine source, also the sahasrara chakra.
The mystery of synchronicity has enveloped us.
The womb of subconscious thought where all things emerge.
Form is extracted from pure madness.
The beginning of infinite possibilities.
The magician exists outside of time.
Before life and after death.

Intereo, graphite on paper, 2011.

Evocative Seclusion

Oh how lovely is the temptation of disassociation
Looking into the black mirror, my reflected self becomes the demon.
Into the world of spirits, the thinning membranes of universes.
Driftings that come unto you and call you with sleepless nights
To their strange lands of twisted architectures and many suns.
The witch can find their way across the path of the moon.
Into the stars we stive with each conjuration of the dark divine.

Evocative Seclusion, pencil on paper, 2013.

Lost in the Path of Totality

Falling down the moon's trail.
The seeker is in darkness.
Child of space, you have forgotten
The purpose of mystery.
My love is the unknowable
Until it is found within the depths of your mind.
Rejoice in the journey of finding
Your way back to bliss or the illusion of sanity.
The adept knows well, we are always on the path.
Embracing the unity of all that is within chaos.
The guide is the silent sun within your core.

Lost in the Path of Totality, drawing from sun and moon phases traced
during eclipse, pencil on paper, 2017.

Voices of Angels

The high of spiritual awakening is a drug so intoxicating
That it corrupts many who dare to play as gods.
The hidden voices will reveal the solvent of evolution
Which is grown within the magus' mind.
By dedication and discipline.
The sacrifice of sacred time.
Through beauteous arts.
That which can not be replicated
Yet is stimulated by evolution
In a sudden revelation and the shifting of aeons.

Voices of Angels, ink on paper, 2018.

Still Alive

The rose is a symbol of death.
Live gracefully and we may hold it in our hands without
disintegrating.
In the ecosystem of self-creation, we grow reality.
Return to the garden.
A flower growing out of my own grave.

Still Alive, ink on paper, 2017.

Process

One's perception of that which terrifies them is based on misunderstanding. Through many incredibly disturbing experiences catalyzed by the pursuit of spiritual freedom and practice, this artist underwent experiences of serious ritual magick through personal study and various occult orders from the age of 18 onwards. Experiments documented through this collection of selected works. Unexplainable horrors manifested, along with wonders beyond description in human understanding - that which normal people would not believe possible to experience in non-fictional or waking reality. That immersion in fear allowed me to make peace with my own mind and realize the power each of us can brandish. I see these works as embracing fear and finding the beauty within. The philosopher's stone in the depths of our shadow self. The artist is the voice of magick and the curator of reality, the curvature of line as the creator of worlds. When all worlds become one, inspiration is limitless and eternal.

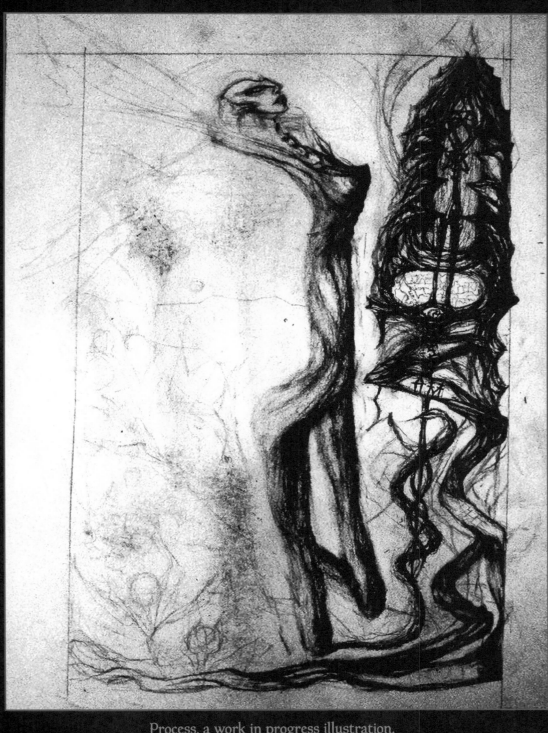

Process, a work in progress illustration,
graphite and pencil on bond paper, 2010.

Orlee Stewart is an occult artist in New Orleans. She was raised in Toronto, Canada in a religious Jewish household and rebelled to become a witch, priestess, exorcist, and consecrated Apostolic and Gnostic Bishop. Orlee is a member of the surrealist Society for Art of Imagination and creates painted spirit portals. Her occult paintings have been exhibited at galleries and events across the world as all her works are enchanted through the powers of magick, carrying gnosis like an event horizon of creativity from the spirit realms. Orlee initially began sharing her occult knowledge as a teacher in secret societies, conducting classes on demonic evocation. She is an Adept of the Esoteric Order of Dagon, Oracle of the Old Ones as well as the Bishop for the Ecclesia Catholica Chaotica Lodge in New Orleans.

Orlee's paintings and illustrations serve as icons to the forces of spiritual energy that exist beyond our world of forms. The purpose of her visionary art is to create an experience for the viewer that will lead to a subjective spiritual awakening. She has had her work published in many grimoires and occult texts while also publishing her own writing and artwork. Orlee's art also manifests into video psychomagick as she studied experimental video arts in university and creates video content about her magical experiments. Orlee's practice is heavily inspired by her relationship with various demonic entities and the spirits of the dead, as well as deities from multiple traditional witchcraft backgrounds.

Orlee does not follow any one set particular system of magick alone, she incorporates paradigms into herself from studying various occult systems and by working with both the forces of light and darkness in union. Orlee has undergone extensive spiritual training for over 15 years to refine her craft and is always learning more. She is trained in Solomanic magick, Tarot Divination, Demonlogy & Excoricm, Necromancy, Folk Witchcraft, and Ceremonial Evocation in Western Theurgy. The motivation behind what Orlee does comes from a deep wish to help inspire the spiritual realms in all those who come into contact with her creative works, to reveal the secrets of the void. Her name literally means "my light" in Hebrew and Orlee wishes to bring light to the mysteries that are hidden deeply within us all.

motherofabominations.com